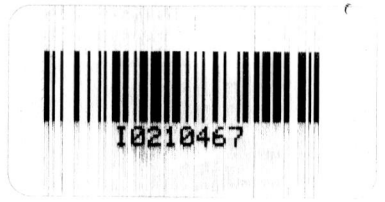

PARALLEL LINES

Also by Dennis Barone

Poetry
The House of Land (Spectacular Diseases, 1986)
Forms / Froms (Potes & Poets, 1988)
Waves of Ice, Waves of Rumor (Zasterle, 1993)
Separate Objects (Left Hand, 1998)

Prose
Abusing the Telephone (Drogue, 1994)
The Returns (Sun & Moon, 1996)
Echoes (Potes & Poets, 1997)
Temple of the Rat (Left Hand, 2000)
The Walls of Circumstance (Avec, 2004)
God's Whisper (Spuyten Duyvil, 2005)
Precise Machine (Quale, 2006)
North Arrow (Quale, 2008)
America / Trattabili (Bordighera, 2011)
Field Report (Quale, 2011)

Editor
The Art of Practice: Forty-Five Contemporary Poets
        (with Peter Ganick) (Potes & Poets, 1994)
Beyond the Red Notebook: Essays on Paul Auster
        (University of Pennsylvania, 1995)
Furnished Rooms by Emanuel Carnevali (Bordighera, 2006)
Visiting Wallace: Poems Inspired by the Life and Work of Wallace Stevens
(with James Finnegan) (University of Iowa, 2009)
Small Towns, Big Cities: The Urban Experience of Italian Americans
(with Stefano Luconi) (American Italian Historical Association, 2010)

Parallel Lines

DENNIS BARONE

Shearsman Books
Exeter

First published in the United Kingdom in 2011 by
Shearsman Books
58 Velwell Road
Exeter EX4 4LD

http://www.shearsman.com/

ISBN 978-1-84861-162-7

Acknowledgements

The author wishes to thank the editors who published much of this
work in magazines, journals, chapbooks, and books. This volume
constitutes a second collection of selected poems, the first, *Separate
Objects*, having been published by Left Hand Books in 1998.

Magazines, etc.: *Abacus, Archeus, Barrow Street, Boundary 2, Cairns, The
Difficulties, Diner, Exquisite Corpse, Generator, The Hartford Courant,
House Organ, Italian Americana, The Love Project, Multiples, The New
Review of Literature, Pages, Paper Air, Paragraph, Paterson Literary
Review, Peregrine, The Poetry Project Newsletter, Some Other Magazine,
Star-Web Paper, Tamarisk, Voices in Italian Americana,*
and *The Wallace Stevens Journal.*

Presses: Philomathean Society, Potes & Poets, Open Township, Quale,
Runaway Spoon, Spuyten Duyvil, Star Cloud, Stride, Talisman, Texture,
University of Iowa, and Writers Forum. On-line: Ekleksographia,
Fiera Lingue, 5 Trope, Italian American Writers, and Poets Press.

Cover: Elizabeth Gourlay *Cello #7*, pencil and acrylic on paper

Contents

Parallel Lines

The Contents

February, a rant interior.
Drinking, smoking, panic, fear.
(Pastoral dialogue:
I ran through the snow like a . . .
a sonnet.)
A guitar. Awake!
A city winter, Saturday afternoon.
A hospital
overlooking the river.
Day and night: the hosts of dreams.
Woman on a beach. Very rainy.
Two epitaphs. Written in January.
to Jane, to the mountains of New York.
elegies, horns of my desire.
Digression: it seems far away.
Anxiety: I will always love you.
To hell with it. Oh, full moon.
In Paris, man with tulip, 1950,
matted and framed, the sad thing
died. I am (whistle) a fine dust.

Or To Know

to have known
or to know by,
at least,
the end of them
(the years)
then to know
what breath is
and to breathe again
safe
in the knowing

The Start of Spring

snow
and a bird's whistle
where was the time
to write
snow
and a bird's whistle
it was
in the spring-
time to write
snow
and a bird's whistle
in the beginning of
spring

I set my bow in the cloud and it shall be a sign.

He planted a vineyard; and he drank of the wine;
and he forgot. Years passed. He grew old and died.
I remember it all because of the sign set in the cloud.
What glistens is not necessarily paramount. This is
also my bow; its colors lack magnificence. But,
read it and know in what direction it points. It
points to its close as the man to his passing.
Here I set my hand against the sign. To be; not to be
remembered— that is the knowledge sought: planted
vines insufficient; clouds exhaustible. To set it
so that the I can be I and not forget. There will
be no sign but all reference in one word, arrow-
like shot from the bow to loop and tie these earthly
words in the drink of the dead man who forgot.

Composition

More than the usual space:
the room and the occupants;
there, breathing space,

instead of tight in a box
now tight in the larger
air of that room.

The Bitter Seeds of Work

We were far from that masonry of the vertical,
the city. Its lattice work was as perfect
as a spider's web. Imagination is a mimic of
the real. "This," I said, "is not real." We
had forgotten the dog patches of York Avenue.
The cry was beneath us when sweat was between
us. With our heaves, our goose-pimples sighed.
I had forgotten your name, but had vowed to
die to prove that you were alive. The city:
that romance of the real, that cyst to pick
thumbnail to thumbnail. "Let's leap,"
I shouted, "to stand at the summit of these
stairs for the stars are impossible when unseen."
"We must remain," you replied, "in ever diminishing
circles." Outside the street urchins stuck to
the sides of bald tires. We hid in each other
and avoided the sun as well as the night. Red
with passion, we reached our peak through prayer
and sweat. Our clocks, once the night owl's hoots,
have become two weak hearts beating. The grass
grows long about our stones. In the gymnasium
you found me practicing for an unnamed war. We
are far from the masonry again. We are free.

Or the thing itself turning into some other

A border so beautiful;
it's crossed with difficulty.
Blooming in fall hardly seems possible.
We are taught, and thus tend to believe, likewise.
Yet, they do bloom white, rose, or red;
in full sun or light shade—
easily. Brilliant;
the blossom is an alternative to the taught.
It is crossed with difficulty,
while the taught is abandoned easily.
Hybrids are deceiving; not always perennial.
The anemone border excludes all others.
Yet, within Saint Brigid's is another circle
and another. There is the circle that is
and the circle that attempts. Together
they achieve, always, others and let
lines such as these mediate between
seed and seed.

Clause for a Uniform Manner of Writing

embrace but one act
and that shall be expressed in the title
title that knows no text
as hand without thumb, grip-less
without opposition
text knows no title that has no opposition
embrace but one act and there will be
never an expression
end the expression that has no title
never begun without the opposition
one act cannot embrace
roots of words that flower
words flower when embraced
no single word alone expresses that embrace
single words are not even titles
names or texts or comments upon them
single words placed on pages at random
cannot express the embrace that flowers
single words placed on pages at random
need the rule of the hand that embraces
the hand that embraces flowers
the hand that embraces flowers
into an expression of the opposition
thumb to forefinger grips
not at empty air but on the image
the image is now one of rabbits
rabbits run down the page
satisfied with the rabbits and the page
and the image of the rabbits on the page
and the *not empty air*, but the image
that grew from the thumb pressed to
forefinger in opposition gripping expression
itself not the title name or comment upon

whether rule governed or at random
was it that the rabbit ate the flower
and left nothing for the author to name and
unnamed the text knew no title
nor what act to embrace?

Types

Cere ves ti
un vem the
teen hun and
O con lad
est con lad
est con O!
Gram the mem
semro arch in
ennor.
Ac mar an
ful mer,
am ward O
ful kie
for ber
for purl
est bohe it!
Mer! Mer!

It was a very sad day

I didn't even know these people
and it's certain they never met one another.
Maybe it was the way the announcements were phrased
or the way they were laid out.
I mean Old Edie, Edie the Egg Lady
was squashed into this tight corner
and she was such a big lady.
She had just had
her teeth "fixed," but the dentist
gave her a set that kept her old
gap so that fans could recognize her.
She didn't even get to use them.
It didn't say which set she was buried in.
And then there was Chester C. Smith,
who I had never even heard of before,
but he was the last, the last
survivor of a police posse that killed
Charles "Pretty Boy" Floyd in 1934.
Saddest thing though, more was said about
Floyd than about Smith. They went on
and on about "most wanted," "notorious,"
"cornered" . . . But
all they said about Smith was that he
retired from the East Liverpool, Ohio
Police Department in 1957.
The day he died was the 50th anniversary of the
slaying of Floyd. Smith shot him dead
on his first try. They didn't say anything
like "Old One Shot Smith" or anything.
I've said more about him than they did.
But the saddest thing by far was
Richard Brautigan, 49; gained
fame in '60s with offbeat novels.

I hadn't even thought about him in 49 years
and apparently neither had anybody else.
His body had been decomposing for two weeks
before some sheriff found it. I suppose
that sheriff is fated to die on the 50th
anniversary of Brautigan's death.
Might be the only way that he'll be
remembered.

Prescriptions

When the pen pushes down on the pad,
indentations form the hieroglyph believed
by generations to be the finished product
of a brilliant mind. What they don't see
are the half-uttered words clipped short,
scratched out and begun again, over and
over. What they don't smell is the oil
leaking from the car that has stopped at
that stop light just long enough to note
that "so much depends." So much depends
upon a moment, a chance encounter, a
phrase or the way Flossie's plums would
have tasted if only he had arrived in time
to take one from the bowl to his lips,
those same lips that utter the words scrawled
across a pad in the morning, typed and
retyped in the evening. Notice
the trace of a hand that existed once.
Follow where it leads.

Pumpkins

Frost might have said the whole place
reeks of them. The very air that we
breathe is rust orange and squash-smell:
putrid to eye and nose. New England,
he might have said mimicking an old
Puritan preacher, stinks in God's nostrils.
You forget this fact about him, about
this place you now call home. Instead of
rot, you think of creation: remember
mom's sweet singing as the pies came
out of the oven on Thanksgiving day
year after year or some coach's cold hand
gripping the back of your neck as he
shoved you on the field to win,
only to win. But Frost wrote more of
loss than victory and in the square
of your village mind, you recall the right
choice made at every fork in the road.
For you day after day begins in sugar,
maple sweet sugar. You think you taste
those pies still, feel the coach's cold hand
even now sending you back to bat, to kick,
to shoot, to stroke, to fire. Memories
like pumpkins decay. Jaded kids of divorced
parentage smash them. Farmers plow them
under to fertilize the fields, a hedge
against next year's loss in the valley of
despair. The little one that ornaments a
desk gets tossed out along with lists
of students' names at term's end. The big
one that's so prized becomes a photograph
lost in a box of photographs. I think
Frost is right: the whole place reeks of them,

rot wins out. I keep some in a box
to smash all year long, to fertilize this garden
that is the blank page. I live here now, too—
in New England amid the pumpkins
and memories the color of rust.

An Ordinary Evening

His house is empty when
He arrives—empty and
Quiet and large. Perhaps,

It is too large for one man
And two women. From
The window of his study

He can look toward the town
He travels to each morning
And returns from each night.

It is winter and the slope of
His yard, so green six months
Ago, is now awash in white,

Patterned slightly by the paws
Of the neighbor's cat. Of the
Garden nothing remains but

The dried out sticks of roses
Trimmed low to the ground
And protruding some above the

Snow. He sits in his study
And thinks of the green of May
And red of June. He awaits

The return of his daughter and
The start of his dinner,
Hearty, he hopes, and hot. He

Dreams the sound of her feet
Upon the stairs, but realizes
That if he has fallen asleep he

Is now awake for she has entered
His room. He smiles,
Stretches forth his hands,

Hands that she steps forward and
Holds. He remembers how
He used to write to her mother

When he went to such distant places
As Greensboro and Elsie stayed
Here at home to guard the fort,

As they used to joke. Holly pulls
Slightly and he stands, shaky
At first, yet, recalling

The hikes he took last spring.

A Passion for Books

There's a book I wrote on the re-shelving
cart. Someone took it out. Someone
returned it. There's no crease along the
spine, no visible marks. Perhaps this
patron did not read it? The other
book of poetry I see is a slim one
from 1943: tattered, worn, well read
and admired—those *Four Quartets*
of Eliot's. Dispirited, I turn to the lobby
Coke machine. I have no quarters, but
I have a dollar. In goes the bill and out
comes my soda. I drink-up; recycle
the can, and return to my book somewhat
revived, my spirits lifted by caffeine
and syrup. I pick up my book and look
at it more closely. One page has been
folded, dog-eared in its upper corner.
It is my least favorite page, the one
about several ordinary spices; the one
that compares cumin, pepper, and sage
to the extraordinary life of Elisha Kent
Kane, the arctic explorer. I return to the
reading room and take my usual position,
that cavernous chair surrounded by
interminable shelves tottering with poetry
and art and science. Doom will come
from neither iceberg nor flood, but
a tremor that'll jolt all these books down
on me and press me between their
bindings like a long-forgotten rose.

While Hearing Mass at Saint Mary's

Nottingham
carried out extensive repairs
there it was
fortress too much
trouble to maintain
artillery too good
no forces other than
two hundred archers
a council meeting on May 12th
and again in September.
An octagonal tower added,
state apartments adjoining
Nottingham, a lively place.
gambling, whoring, and
the attempt to impose a
closing time ridiculed.
Edward and Richard met there.
Edward stayed for weeks,
and, not too sure of his popularity,
gave up and turned south.
Some associate Richard's "castle
of his care" with the octagonal
tower and the castle as being "in
his care." Later,
Richard decreed:
"they be of timber instead of stone."
Comfort replaced defense.
Well-lit rooms, wainscoted and tapestried;
molded ceilings and carved beams,
great stone chimney-pieces with
cheerful open hearths.
Edward was dead.
Friday, September 11th—

the arrival of the ambassadors.
Peace, under an emblazoned canopy.
Back at Nottingham
on the following Tuesday night,
Richard slept. On Wednesday,
he hunted. News arrived
and he left frowning;
mounted on a great white
courser. Great was the
lamentation of the people at
his going. After the battle,
he heard Mass at Saint Mary's.

Conceptions

and what words
fill the gaps

disconnection and disruption

in the process of
investigation (no answers)

who says?

say
our money evenly divided
a clean sheet
cleared of imbalance

the mountains in spring
lifted to new heights
this is hyperbole
a straight line and a single tone
that is truth
what did you make of it?
the parapet

we packed the car
what else was there?
in the desert—the sand
and beyond, the tower

it was all a mystery
the muddy, unpaved streets

had survived the mid-point
had entered the wilderness
had prayed to something

photos of people
faces in the photos
the church of something-left-behind

wire to us
photographs of us
we have survived

Eternity

wave Greece cartilage
refuse or boat to
transport send place
fishing a dam a fence
set in Polynesian
people unconscious in
abstract world not trans
cendent aroused by
experience habit things
in themselves project
on nature wind rain
run in childbirth re
ward sublime deep mud
mire moral cast off irk
some body and meter both
decorative (horse) adorn
habit shape

Blue Tiger

This is the story of a vegetarian pacifist
who steals all the turkeys from a New England Inn
and buries them in the town's war cemetery
located behind the town hall just off
the village green.

This is the story of a twenty-four hour
personal Jesus, flexible salvation hours guaranteed!

Push button to restart. In Connecticut it is
raining all the time or it isn't.

Did you see the new ad for the Popeil
Pocket Popcorn Popper on the Christian Cartoon Network
yet?

Why is the freezer so cold?

This is the story of Joseph Priestley,
who discovered oxygen and then is reported
to have said: it is impossible to write
on air. Whatever you say disappears.

Spring

Displays of difference are sanctioned only when
they provide a multicultural spectacle.

add one green pepper to the above

This is the story of so many repetitions
and so many connections,

even small ones of single words
such as "batten" and "tile."

add one green pepper to the above

Things begin to change when problems
begin to occur. We have no national
tree.

The Fiction of Authenticity and Authentic Fiction

The Sherry Netherland, New York

This is the story of
Press button to restart
In Connecticut it is
Add one green pepper

dappled

Advice: if you're going to get
sick you might as well get sick
when you're injured.

The Church of the Twenty-Four Hour Personal Jesus
(Flexible Salvation Hours Guaranteed)

This is the story of playing catch-up
with the list-serve, reading the thought of
thousands strewn global now reduced
to the mere pinhead of this screen and
its pixels. Whose Chicago?

Busy, I'm not racing today,
just running.

Why fall behind when you can get ahead?
Call the New Jersey Re-Finance Authority
today

Don't stammer. Try to
think of everyone, not just
a single one.

Whose Chicago
The Church of the

Busy, I'm not

This is the story of the prompter. I'm
quite fond of the prompter.

Spring.

The retrenched lines of domestic discovery

I will forever keep before the reader's
eye the ingenious could be.

This is the story of playing catch-up
with the list-serve, reading Joseph
Priestley's axiom: "Your resolution
must appear," he wrote

The focus is on the horse,
the geography of relationships;
selected conference activity.

"Your resolution must
appear," he wrote, "a natural progression;
not a shocking imposition."

Can more use be made of the smell of their
breath, the shape of their hats?

The Sherry Netherland
The Network
24 Hours

Although the focus is on the horse as
an animal of noble recreation, the working
horse is not neglected.

This is the story of the town hall
just off the village green

This is the story of the robot arm
and the restart button and one
green pepper outside in the rain
or it isn't.

Shifting Point

We view it
through action and dialogue.

Their gold sin
they've learned lies dead.

Yet what they
did fate willed and planned.

He knew it
and uttered his final boast.

The last survivor
not from desire but need.

Then darkness
loud tongued forgot the future glory.

What must be
gives useless weapons.

The singer finished
turned fate aside in smiles.

He shaped it
bewitched, laid spells, blunted fate.

He stripped
pleased as the sun had gone.

What was right
if your hands were hard?

No one could
unwind in friendship, reception.

Scorn and
sometimes grace in a world.

Champion that
the ways his eyes want.

It sounded
almost dagger-like.

Inside an apron
and the people were afraid.

Start it here
dead ones: Adam's apple,

everything.

Poem

Words matter.

Insert a comma,
a tack
to pin it down.

A king rules
and rules,
a king.

Who Gives Us the Name

moving as the body does
the trees and the web
suspended in front of them
in front of them
the whirling insects fly
in haphazard directions
one-hundred thousand of them
at least line the shore
to watch the changing of the tide
a fragment broken off from silence
words as children of the silence
no one or two of them can fix
but all of them must suggest

write this

we hold the password,
a recurrent one
name
one-hundred thousand of them at least
no one or two of them can fix
but all of them must suggest
the way a body moves
through that middle distance
where all the life is

Exploration of the Frontier

Waist-high in bright fresh color—could they forget the failure?
Salt-tang in the air with all cool profusion.
Audubon lived constantly with the knowledge of that very
        grandeur.
Waist-high in bright fresh color—could they forget the failure?

A thousand images—and ideas and plans, the end of splendor.
Coronado's was not the only solution.
Waist-high in bright fresh color—could they forget the failure?
Salt-tang in the air with all cool profusion.

What does it matter?

All Saturday afternoon
the clown drifts. I am
not sure there is
a cure. Should we
think of Canada or
another card? The sun
near what appears to be
the young Christ? Wind?
What does it matter?
A certain person and
then a tornado, a ribbon
far away? She has
lunch only it's boring
at night and tomorrow
morning a child takes
off through alfalfa and
you are tired of light.
Do not toss the haze
—dark, wet—down
the alley. Black trees:
I get up in blood, have
to smile that there's
a city where I lost days.
What does it matter?
Who takes the sea
and laughs briefly, gets
up, paces the blue rug
and comes in your
raincoat to the reclining
limp edge of a cure,
a taxicab here in the dust?
I cannot possibly

guide you down there
around the sea of kindness.
The lame dog changes
plans and I am happy.
What does it matter?
The snow in clear
light sometimes does
reach you, an armory
for a moment. If only
people looked glad
that this particular
harvest has suddenly
got to you. You should be
writing on pewter something
grand, a little island;
a piano of gold.
Escape the gray end
of desire! Protest
the room although it
sounds better to be
an angel. Oh,
in the fall I tried
to tell you of disaster,
some great sadness,
tons of it.
What does it matter?
You passed over the painful
excitement. Our masks
are more beautiful than
the apple, the cinema,
the clouds, the cold snow,
the clown's. Around me
heat rises, dreams.

Light comes on, reaches
down and the black sky
in your lids streams
through the dark red
inside me.
What does it matter?
There were fronds
heavy in a town
by the sea.
I hear the old door,
the young Christ.
They stretch and we
are tired. The walls
hardly ever hold.
We've got to give
the oaks more than
night! Whole days
go by and we
arouse the harbor,
walk into a theater.

What Lasts

There is a reason for all the ripples
and the still protests beyond.
There is a reason for vacancies in the sky;
a reason for dark objects
that mark and configure a shore.

The reason is this:
one frayed rope of light
binds persistent space and ties
the ocher curl of a final cockspur
leaf to that rippled surface.

Humming

The orange peel from the morning
still on the back of the tongue.
Dry chalk and banana in
the air of the room, cold air
that makes little mountains
on the palm. Everything turns
green: the valleys, the ridges along-
side. Words to be written,
green words and orange
and the time in which to write
them and the air to breathe
and the breath so necessary
to say them.

The Surface of Things

What is the story behind
Those dots beside the black
Marks on the white paper?

What if?
And then . . .
And then . . .

Today I held a human heart in my hands
And then I cut it apart. "Hark!" it cried
Having meant to have cried, "Hank?"

A robot nails shut its box
The boy sits in his room
The boy looks at a picture book

The boy cannot leave his room

Living Room

The word *family* has come to mean
Fewer and fewer people

I myself am the emblem of the form

Rhyme, a word to end the line
But not the sentence

The blue of the eyes
Is not the blue of the sea

Why is the child a gleam
In the father's eyes

Fit a mold and be
Remodeled

Parenting

We chose not to
It wasn't an easy decision
Often I daydream
But never incessantly
I want to be precise
This doesn't keep me
Awake at night
And yet
Can you imagine?

Improbable Wave

Our rooms are
alpine. He had the child
and the truth. You too
approached the window
as if a small room
dreamed nothing.

At night
he could not bolt
cars to the highway.
The baby climbed from the road,
closed the piers—deaths
everywhere.

From this distance
an apprenticeship cannot
square the bus into
a place difficult now
to speak of—

the house.

Each dawn
a flat sea
ruined the trees—
he says
the hills *sing*

(near your eyes

to reduce the casual
hours
of beautiful water

in that light).

Outside

parked in the fields
silence indeed
lies hip high.

A bird, someone
cobbled in a poor
district.

This is accepted:
the constant darkness
of drunken men,

stone towers
issuing sorrow.

The eye is old and
there is no other guarantee.

The hard world is troubled,
pressed—hiding words.

Docudrama

A window repairman came to repair
a window where a bird had flown
into it and broke it. The next day another
bird met its match on the window's mate.

Poetry is the absence of insurance.

In another room another man spoke about a woman
in a language that could not be understood and he
kept close count of his pulse as he struck the ivory
keys on an out-of-tune piano and remembered.

Poetry is the absence of insurance.

An Interrogation of the Moon

Perforce must begin with less posturing
Not to be confused with backslap
You must rejoice in language
What are inches let us dance the
Tarantella you take care of everything
And start to live you made supper you
May wonder what to hang on walls
You may feel that you have
Neglected the garage don't be
Fooled by relationships are crucial
A sofa and a chair you can't
Have pools of light people brought things
With them we should have a quiet
Place some towels for a spill and
A phone to ring with an orange
Commedia at the top of a hill

Field Report

four angles
a form of wisdom for the flight

conventionalized
the diagram illustrating the wheel

crows
being further from society
would not have understood

promises
a special dye

derived
from the written word
but used no longer

a prophet
laid down the border
and followed the road of broken stone

a palace
in brown calf-skin

in flour
the thread went north

they performed in masks
the course of the book

A Sentimental Education

sat on a chair
between high buildings
minutes passed and
sad, but an aunt
somewhere else started
up hope to charm
miserable eyes
ten past four
others offered to lead
in silence
I went over, had
lost the privilege
huge house / express train
all the most polished
surroundings a little
miserable
lack sufficient cash
each little girl
to believe
each tiresome house
had such hope for
an afternoon
to carry from the stage
but ill-starred
in the show slipped
and the spell cut—
our fear locked in each
anticipation of night
without sleep
half-expected lamps
an embarrassment,
ever-on and
the darkness of air
touched, made to weep

Scarf

He asked,
"And the fishes
who keep being silent;
do they mean it?"
He could hum
even when crippled
"Ain't We Got Fun."
One night high in a dark
jewel of a place
he slashed at slow—
going hours.

For a time, details
transfixed that awkward
sky. He got the call—
"look, I love you"
—but refused to answer.

There are other hungers
than those for warm weather,
free days.

Statistically
there isn't much we
can say.

Because the lands are so
large the stories must be
short—to unify and predict.

Several members of our
committee demanded more
comfortable hotel rooms

to facilitate their aesthetic
judgment.

This camera is not alert.
a clause in a sentence
a clause in a memorable sentence
a sentence in a short story
a sentence in a story by a
forgotten writer
a clause in a sentence a story
memorable but unread
unread because the writer has been
forgotten, obscured
remember how he worked
for his own obscurity
and that of others
he devoted his life to his own
obscurity and that of others
some of the others on occasion
may be recalled thanks
to his efforts while he
is not

In the dawn he wakes
His camera is not alert
A man stands by
an open window
Does he yawn or does he sing?

"John, come here. Look at my feet."
"What is it, dear?"
"See that toe?"
"Which one?"

"The third one. See it?"
"Which foot?"
"The right one."
"What is it?"
"You see it?"
"Yes."
"Well?'
"What is it? What am I supposed to see?"
"That toe."
"What about it?"
"That toe. It is not mine."
"What?"
"That toe is not my toe."
"Well whose is it?"
"I don't know. I just noticed it—that it's not mine, I mean."
"It looks like yours."
"No. No, mine was different."
"In what way, dear?"
"In every way, John."
"How do you know?"
"Just look at it, John. Just look at it. It isn't me. It isn't mine."
"Are you sure? I don't . . ."
"Yes, I'm sure."
"Well, then. There's only one thing to do."
"I know. I thought so, I mean."
"We'll have to remove it. You'll have to lose the toe before we lose all of you."
"I'm ready now. Go and get your saw. I will still be here when you return."

At my present age
he was already seven
years dead.

"If I had a dog, John, I'd
name her Spout. 'Down,
Spout. Down, Spout'."

Perhaps we should think in terms
    of opera?

The sports star's fall from grace
    or the politician's rise to power?

What seems to be the problem, Officer?

Bones are / the die is

Something small holds on to a leg,
cheek pressed tight to that leg.

And then is dragged …

But then wondered if it was all too
much by rote, free of all emotion
and connection, a repetition
emptied of all meaning.

—can you use the first part as a frame?

the bulldozers are always at work

  stone, an object, a fragment of rock

mornings worked themselves onto the street

the window, the interlocking branches
the necessary steps and stairs
any particular pine
a representational figure
a street where a photographer may flash an image

no romance when bony hands
tell fortunes

and keep open the communal wound

the supermarket across the street

variations in color
and texture

absence of demand
clouded activation

the most marginal
foothills

the true black of
fabrication

the end of glint,
a fading odyssey

to write
today a memo
tomorrow a monument

to right
wrongs
left over from previous
writings

What does this word say?
I cannot read it.

It says: "communicate."

when it comes to a storm
we have good reason to howl

—a euphemism for survival.

a false distinction

one merely dramatizes results

he says sings prays sings shouts
he asks he crosses doubt
he rhymes and finds warmth there
momentarily

the nature of the stone
   dictates the cut

said to be highly skilled and

well qualified for the task

The dozers will groan
as they strike every side,
reducing all to rubble.

White space:
the tragedy of unrecorded
events.

a thin and porous line
between humor and horror

He is a moralist.

perplexed by a benevolent overflow
of ideas

It is a topic,
not necessarily a *position*,
he said.

"I am not at war,"
he said.

"I am not at war—
a fact, not a bumper sticker."

It was for the victors
that Pindar wrote his odes.

Embrace on the bus
whoever is next to you,
he said.

it seems

(There is little evidence to clarify

We've written what we want to read.

Such phrases as these—
"have pity"; "have mercy," were
frequently intermingled with groans,
and accompanied with weeping.

His brain appeared to suffer
some severe constriction.

He desired to be excused,
for a few minutes, from proceeding.

There is little evidence to clarify

My hands hold onto the notebook.

I reach out for the hands of the other
and the notebook closes.

Che Tempo

Un po' nuvoloso,
dappertutto.
Sono l'uccello.
Dove sono
i nostri
amici?
Quando
rientreranno?
Dappertutto,
un po' nuvoloso.

Loro Dimenticano

un solo pensiero
loro capiscono

un solo pensiero
loro dimenticano

le città sono deserte
fa freddo in questa casa

non ci sono . . .
ma ci sono . . .

deve essere
fiori nei giardini

loro dimenticano
oggi, la luna storta

In Quest' Albergo

Il capocameriere dice:
"Ma che bella giornata, oggi!"
Sorride con tenerezza.
Il capocameriere dice:
"Pioverà oggi!"
Aggrotta le sopracciglia con grazia.
Ecco i suoi saluti, ogni mattino.
A ogni signora anziana,
E ogni signore anziano,
E ogni canaglia incallita,
E ogni coppia giovane—
A ogni ospite.

Ed io, che non dormo, resto qui in attesa e scruto l'alba,
Un giorno scenderò giù nel mondo
E allora avrò una tromba potente come il vento,
E strombazzerò fuori dal mondo
Lo splendido luogo comune:
"Ma che bella giornata, oggi!"
E un altro giorno urlerò disperato,

"Pioverà oggi!"
Per ogni signora anziana,
E ogni signore anziano,
E ogni canaglia incallita,
E ogni coppia giovane—
Non sono forse ospiti in quest' albergo,
Dove il cielo è il soffitto
E il pavimento è la terra,
E le stanze sono le case?

Ma io, io—povero disgraziato—
Potrei chiedere un lavoro

Come capocameriere
Di quest' albergo?

(after Emanuel Carnevali)

Musica

Cielo azzurro.

Altrove:
mari mossi.

so-la-ti
so-la-ti-do

Music

Blue sky.

Elsewhere:
rough seas.

so-la-ti
so-la-ti-do

April

Here I am!
Can I speak to you?
Is it possible?
Why not?
For sale,
my heart—
with polka-dots!
What are you doing?
Hurry! Hurry!

Mask

Yesterday I went to Bologna.
I made the situation worse.
I climbed the stairs.
Times have changed.

Times have changed.
I went by the house last night.
I had already finished my work.
Before going out, I turned off the lights.

Before going out, I turned off the lights.
I spent my summer at the beach.
I wasn't able to return as planned.
Yesterday an occurrence developed in Bologna.

Yesterday something happened in Bologna.
I wasn't able to understand it.
I ran to the house.
Giorgio Morandi died at midnight.

Ruins

It is as if thick fog
kept the morning from
reaching us. A crowd of

hands lost here in an image
or dream that we believed would
lift shadows; reveal light.

We wait for the cloud to break
outside, to play again as before
beyond the walls in a bright wood,

but there remains uncertainty
and in the emptiness all
passes as the birds above.

We said it was too long,
circling in the dark. A prayer,
wild as love, lived on such

sayings as told in the dark.

(after Carlo Betocchi)

Map

A song of bridges
And then a silence

At one time
There were no stones

Oak rippled water
And an oar-less boat

At night: darkness
As expected; then morning

A wing that beats
The silence back

Perspective

True poetry reveals itself by its
capacity to free us. That's
what Goethe said, but the police officer
didn't hear my poet friend's words
when the latter pleaded, "you've
got the wrong man, Sir." My friend spent
three nights in jail. I am
convinced that this poet
indeed is a very good one
and the policeman, a very bad officer of the law,
mixed in all that mud you sometimes
read about or hear on the news
knowing so well you remain
so high above that you'd never
be pulled down, even if you had
the urge to let go of your balloon and let the
cop have it right in the kisser as
he reaches—wrongfully—for your
thunderstruck arm.

Perfect Six

History is the end of all things eternal.
The a-historical bee never exits the hive.
We remember Achilles. Then recall that
He died. Sometimes we can glimpse
The pacing, the placing of our returns from
The theoretical to the autobiographical.
A door may open: the thing to do is enter.

Lid

He would entertain us in the evening with the recitation
of his beloved poems.

Boom ca trot zir: veer a mi static bat.
Propensity devolve hab: murnot, ripod heme.
Cornlot, trot megantun, havel zeel oberstopant.
Crabor librumot boom ca triffel peet. Toreems
Vagabond scree, platus fat, evermore zir fulcrum stat.
Overland scree hab otto zir mi offenhat.

Boom ca allenzart nar axron nar catten rumb.
Havekir allentar mir trot nex, fumen catencomb:
Al-noxlay halen zir, may kottunen allenback.
Oberhandon drawtoon al-boom scree infeltant.
Platus-rec gamu-tec: offen al havel nar pullenbus.
Ovidloon bugton, landtrot, zir boom undertruss.

Have carem boom ca, have carem tundra heer;
Have careem zirzout, lindensteer trot mi offenteer.

Great Expectations

A funnel hat
A furnace of knowledge
Authoritative
As all that
Industry
Its weight
At his command

His train

All in black

Draped

He had a hat
He wore it on his head,
A big hat
And he had a beard

He had a deep voice
He was smart
And he was good
And he had a beard

He came from the mid-west
He died in the east
And he had a beard

Many people saw the train
The train stopped in many towns
The train that brought him home
Was long and dark
Just like his beard

If he was so smart
Why was his speech so short
If he was a man of the people
Why was he the tallest person around

Legacy

Efficiency is the death of poetry.
A foundation survives to
Reveal such small dimension.
Our skeletons grow
Weary and other voices start
Singing X Y Z,
X Y Z. Memory remains
Intimate. The clock strikes:
Cakes we called "the fingers
Of the Holy Apostles." We lived
Close fisted and greedy of filthy
Lucre: efficient. And I
Hesitate to say this but
(and repeat over and over again

Here are the stones

Where are the workers?
Stones remain.
A line of hammers struck
but the workers left
for the suburbs.
Here are the stones.
Where are the workers?
The owner paid well
—carver and quarryman—
took care of them
when they got sick. God bless
him. Here
are the stones. Where
are the workers?
Stones cut workers inside
out. Workers cut stones
outside in. Trees reclaim
yards and beds. The dead
below rest without
memorial or marker, far
from any suburb elysian.
But the owner lives on:
in town, school, street, store,
and more. Our guide says:
he was a kind God.

Breathless

The clock struck two
and then the ants came,
tiny assassins holding us
down. Soon our
breath became the shallow
end of a sea, a fire
slowly extinguishing itself,
a final blow in the grip
of a hurricane.

The Big Push

The radius never expanded
And the planet always
Circled the sun, but at

Age twenty-four, one
Doesn't feel it turning.
Then—all of a sudden—

At age sixty, one stands
Still and senses that larger
Movement; thinks then

There are no answers.
The fact of an address does
Not solve the situation.

Names change. Memory
Finds a place to live
In the barren gray woods

Of December. My tent has
Been pitched. I'll row
A canoe down the river

Just so I can recall its name.
Some say the neighbors are
Unfriendly, more reticent

Than any Mayflower descendant.
Let silence enlarge and keep us
All as clean as snow.

Air Flow

any rose illuminates
but some have broken and
others have been removed

yellow and blue and green
water marks itself for pleasure
something is immovable, inanimate

love is anxious in those soft
clouds in those sweet, sweet
sounds taking elephants along

lungs have been fed wind
emptied, put on a closet shelf—
door left open for investment

at rates favorable love
offers roses, or any flower of any
color, well-watered, alive

Parallel Lines

A ladder's steps. Jacob's
ladder. Black on white.
Clasped hands. Vacant.
Boundary not straight,
no sound: no pulsation.

Recall a rooster. A rooster
made of lines, curving
lines (there are no
straight lines in nature).
Recall a rooster: next
door, also framed.
A frame is not a field,
a field of lines within the frame:
ten parallel lines, matted
and in a brown frame
far from the rooster's call, so
quiet is the rooster so framed.

So framed the rooster makes
no call, no call in the morning,
early in the morning and we
are glad and we are thankful
for the quiet, the absence of the
call, call, call. So quiet here
on the white sheets in this
bed on the brown rug in the
room, a rectangle, in the house
also framed now on four
sides by a white fence that
appears at this hour dark
and quiet and dark and glad
upon the bed two lines not

climbing, not climbing the ladder.
Two lines not parallel not
not touching, but intertwined.

www.ingramcontent.com/pod-product-compliance
Lightning Source LLC
Chambersburg PA
CBHW031929080426
42734CB00007B/611